Dear Reader,

How do girls like you handle everyday problems? We wanted to find out. So we posted the questions in this book on the American Girl Web site. Thousands of girls responded, offering great solutions and practical advice on dealing with difficult situations.

Now it's your turn. *What Would You Do?* is filled with dilemmas most girls face sooner or later. Each problem is followed by three different solutions. Choose the response that most closely matches what yours would be. Then find out what that choice says about you.

While you might not have the power to control what happens on the outside—at school, at home, or with friends—you can always control what happens on the inside. You do this by making choices that are right for you. We hope this book will help you do just that.

Your friends at American Girl

Contents

Family Matters

What role do you have in your family? Are you the one starting the arguments or trying to end them? Are you the one who keeps everyone laughing or keeps them in line? Whatever your role, your family wouldn't be the same without you.

1. Your sister always barges into your room without knocking. It's annoying!

What would you do?

☐ a. Set some rules—now

Every time my sisters barged into my room, I made them give me ten cents. Soon I had a pretty big profit and they started knocking.
Jodie, age 12, SC

☐ b. Talk it out

Explain how you feel. If she still does not respect your privacy, then call a family meeting and find a way to fix the problem.
Lucy, age 12, United Kingdom

☐ c. Let it go

She most likely wants to hang out with you, so instead of getting mad at her, hang out with her.
Jessica, age 12, UT

2.

■ You and Mom haven't been getting along lately. You seem to fight about everything! You'd really like to talk to her about growing up, but you can barely talk about the weather without having an argument.

What would you do?

☐ a. Write her a note

My mom and I write to each other in a journal. If I have a question that I feel awkward asking in person, or if I want to apologize for getting into an argument, I write to her in the journal that we share.
Becki, age 12, OH

☐ b. Have a heart-to-heart talk

Sit down with your mom and say, "Mom, things have been really tense. I want to be able to talk to you, but we always fight." Hopefully, you'll be able to talk it through.
EB, age 13, WA

☐ c. Don't sweat the small stuff

Remind yourself not to get so mad over little things, and that way you won't get into so many arguments.
Elies, age 15, MI

3. Your mom always promises to do things with you, then cancels at the last minute. You're starting to feel as if she doesn't even want to spend time with you.

What would you do?

a. Make time
My mom and I decided to set aside the same day of the week, every week, for spending time together.
Taza, age 11, NJ

b. Be honest
Tell your mom how you feel. Maybe she doesn't know that it hurts your feelings. Tell her that you know she is busy but that sometimes you would like her to take time off and have some fun with you.
Adri, age 11, KS

c. Cut her some slack
Never think that your mom doesn't love you. It's just that her job takes time. Maybe you can help out around the house. That will give her more time to spend with you.
Kelsey, age 11, NJ

4. School just let out for break, and you and your brother are already fighting. You don't want to spend the whole vacation fighting with him.

What would you do?

☐ **a. Tell your mom**

If your brother starts bugging you for no reason, tell him that if he doesn't stop, you'll tell your parents. Don't put up with it!
Brett, age 11, CA

☐ **b. Call a truce**

Talk to your brother, and tell him you're sick of fighting and want to make up. You're lucky to have a brother, even if you don't always get along. You never know—maybe he feels the same way but is too shy to say anything.
Ashley, age 12, IL

☐ **c. Get on his good side**

Try to do something really nice for him; that way he can't be mean. Walls between people build up brick by brick, and they come down the same way!
Taya, age 12, CA

5. ■ Your sister constantly leaves her things all over the house and never cleans up. She also won't do her share of the chores. You ask her nicely to put her things away, but she doesn't. You've told your parents what's happening, but they don't agree. You don't think they realize how much of her work you're doing.

What would you do?

☐ a. Do only your share

Your sister probably knows that if she doesn't do the work, eventually you will. Just do your share of the work and let her see how messy she is. Your parents might notice, too.

Derrina, age 14, FL

☐ b. Call a family meeting

State your problem clearly to your parents and your sister. "I think it's unfair I'm doing so much work. It gets frustrating when everything is so messy and I'm doing her share of the chores. Can we work something out?" Work hard to find a solution, and be patient.

An American girl

☐ c. Make it fun

Make your sister's chores a game! When washing the dishes, pretend your sister is Cinderella, held captive until she finishes the job. When putting away toys, your sister is a princess who wants to marry Prince Clean-Me-Up, but before that, she must put away all the toys.

An American girl

Tally your answers here:

a's_____ **b's**_____ **c's**_____

Mostly a's—Perfectly Practical

You're known as the go-getter of the family, and you like a good challenge. Your sibs think you're competitive. Your friends call you intense. Order and routine are important to you. When a leader is needed, you're ready to take control and get things done. But you may end up disappointed if you expect others to keep up with your hurried pace.

Conflict doesn't scare you, and nothing's better than a healthy debate around the dinner table. You have no problem getting your point across. When it's time to listen, however, you find that's easier said than done. Remember, it's important to be understood, but it's equally important to understand the other person's point of view.

Mostly **b**'s—Talk It Out

At the end of the day, you love nothing more than to flop down on your bed with your mom for a long chat. You are sensitive and caring, and when it comes to the way others are feeling, you've got great instincts. You tend to be affectionate and loving with those closest to you, and you're willing to compromise when you need to.

You look for ways to solve conflicts in a way that works for everyone. Family conflicts really upset you.

You want to talk it out until things feel better. Be sure to say what's on your mind, even if it means writing a person a letter. You may be disappointed if you don't get the response you want, but you need to accept that this happens. It doesn't mean the person doesn't care. Remember, just because people understand where you're coming from doesn't mean they'll agree with you. Find a creative way to express your feelings, like writing in a journal.

Mostly C's—Peacekeeper

You have a carefree approach to life. You can be silly with your sibs and bring laughter to the family table. Living with you is easy because of your playful nature. Your family is important to you, and you show them by helping out and doing special things for them. You have a giving spirit, even when it means you miss out. You're happy to go with the flow.

When there's conflict in your family, you'll either dismiss it or patch things up ASAP. But sometimes, tough stuff really needs to be talked about. Make sure your own needs are met, and ask for time or attention when you need it. Know that you can be a "team player" and still be true to yourself.

Friends

Making and keeping friends is not always easy. At times, you'll feel torn between what to do to keep yourself happy and how to keep your friends happy, too. The most important thing to remember is that part of being a good friend is being honest—with your friends and with yourself.

1. You have two friends who hate each other. One says, "If you hang around her, I'm not your friend."

What would you do?

☐ **a.** Set her straight

Tell your friend that you like the other girl just as much as you like her, and that you will not ditch the other girl just because your friend threatens not to like you anymore. If this friend doesn't understand, then you might be better off without her for a friend.

Katie, age 12, MA

☐ **b.** Be sensitive

Whenever you're with one of your friends, don't mention it to the other one. Whenever my best friend tells me about the fun stuff that she and her other friends do, it makes me madder and madder. Also, see if you can find something that both your friends have in common.

Tracy, age 12, MI

☐ **c.** Give it time

I've been a friend in the middle before. I just gave the situation time and my friends grew on each other. Show them what they have in common to get them started.

Laura, age 13, NY

2. One of your best friends told you a mean lie. You asked her if she wanted to sleep over and see a movie. She told you she couldn't. But when you went to the movie alone, you saw her there with someone else.

What would you do?

☐ **a. Get angry**

Confront your friend and tell her you saw her at the movies. Ask her why she lied. Tell her that you would have understood if she had already made plans and that you'd appreciate it if she would be honest next time.
Amanda, age 12, MI

☐ **b. Get the whole story**

Maybe there was a misunderstanding. Your friend might have promised another friend that she would go to the movie before you asked her. Continuing to be angry with your friend isn't going to solve anything, so you should talk to her.
Christine, age 13, MI

☐ **c. Give her a break**

Don't be mad. Your friend probably already had plans with the girl you saw her with at the theater. She most likely told the lie to avoid hurting your feelings. She might have been telling the truth in some way or another!
Danielle, age 9, PA

3. Recently, you got a cool black leather jacket as a gift. As soon as your friend found out about it, she bought exactly the same one before you had a chance to wear it to school and be the only one wearing it. Then you got a charm for your charm bracelet, and she bought the same one.

What would you do?

☐ a. Lay it on the line

Tell her that you try hard to be original and you don't appreciate it when you end up looking just like her. She should realize how important your style is to you.

Allie, age 13, TX

☐ b. Take her shopping

Go shopping with her one day and help her pick out things. She might need a little boost, and you're the perfect person to give it.

Ann, age 13, MN

☐ c. Have fun with it

Some of my friends do exactly the same thing. Instead of thinking that they copied me to be mean or selfish, I think of how much they look up to me and how much they like me as a good friend. Pretend you are twins, and just hang out and have fun.

Margaret, age 13, NC

4. Your new friend talks about your other friends whenever they aren't around! You have a problem with that, and you're worried that she talks about you when you're not around.

What would you do?

☐ **a. Defend your friends**

Next time she talks about someone else, remind her that others have feelings and tell her to stop. If she continues, just walk away.
Natalie, age 10, OH

☐ **b. Talk to her**

Try talking with her about it. Maybe she's not trying to be mean. Maybe she just wants to know everyone better and learn everyone's opinion. She's new, so don't be too hard on her.
Agnieszka, age 14, IL

☐ **c. Be positive**

Think on the positive side. If one of your other friends is mentioned in a conversation, talk about her good qualities and what you like about her. Don't say mean things.
An American girl

5. Whenever one of your friends does something better or has a cuter outfit than you do, you get so jealous that you say mean things about her. You really don't want to feel so jealous, but you can't seem to stop.

What would you do?

☐ **a.** Look inside

You have your own style and personality. No one is perfect. When a friend does something better than you, it's just another goal to accomplish—getting better at something.
An American girl

☐ **b.** Be happy for her

I get jealous too, but I feel happy for my friends, because they have such nice things, and I don't want to be mean to them. I'll say, "I like that. Where'd you get it?" Then, if I want to get it, I'll know where to go!
An American girl

☐ **c.** Be creative

Make a "My Good Qualities" journal. Take a notebook and write down all the good things you can think of about yourself. Take a look at your journal when you get jealous.
Alex, age 9, CA

Mostly **a**'s—Chief Chum

When you walk through the halls at school, people know who you are. You're a girl who's not afraid to speak her mind, especially when the subject is something you feel passionately about. You are strong-willed and won't be pushed around by others. And you won't let your friends be pushed around either. You're a loyal friend and a leader. The bottom line is you like to be in control, which is a real strength, unless you are trying to control your friends.

Make sure you give others a chance to express themselves, and listen to what they have to say. Although compromising might not come naturally to you, it's worth working on. You'll enjoy your friendships more and earn the true respect you're looking for.

Mostly b's—Heart & Soul Sister

You're a girl who loves having friends. Hanging out with them is your favorite way to spend the day. Relationships mean a lot to you, and you work to keep those around you happy. You're a good listener with a kind heart, and your friends rely on you for support and encouragement.

When trouble hits, you work very hard to make things right as soon as possible. Holding a grudge isn't your style, and you easily forgive, even if you're still really hurting inside. You always try to be nice and are known for your flexibility and willingness to help. Just be sure you aren't trading away your own happiness in order to belong. You need to know when to say "enough is enough," especially when friends cross the line by lying or telling your secrets. Remember that friendship is a two-way street, and it's O.K. to say when something isn't working for you.

Mostly C's—Free Spirit

You're as down-to-earth as they come. Instead of "sweating the small stuff," you look for a different perspective or a better way. Creative and fun-loving, you enjoy being with friends, but you also like to spend time alone. Being your friend is easy, because you're accepting of others' strengths and weaknesses. You're patient and have a positive attitude.

When faced with a conflict, you're likely to withdraw and wait for things to cool down. You're not afraid to go your own way, which is a strength. Just be sure you are letting your friends really get to know you. Share your thoughts and opinions with them. And don't be afraid to stand up for yourself when someone stomps on you. Honesty will deepen your friendships and make them more meaningful.

Decisions, Decisions

Like most kids, you probably want to "do the right thing," but what happens when the right thing isn't clear? Do you live by the letter of the law, or does a more flexible approach work for you? Does decision making in general make you nervous, or do you welcome the challenge? Turn the page to find out . . .

1.

Your best friend keeps pressuring you to do things that your parents wouldn't want you to do. When you tell her that you're not allowed, she says something like, "They'll never know," or "I guess I'm not important enough to you." You don't want to lose her friendship, but you're not sure you can take it anymore.

What would you do?

☐ a. Tell her off

Say, "Look, if you really are my friend, why are you pressuring me to do things I don't want to do? It's really annoying, and I wish you would stop it." Don't be mean; just be blunt. She'll get the message.
Angelina, age 14, NY

☐ b. Use humor

I know what you are going through because I have a friend who's always telling me to do something I shouldn't. I always tell her no and give her a funny excuse. She always laughs and ends up forgetting about it.
Laura Beth, age 12, SC

☐ c. Hit the road

Just get a new friend. It will save you from getting into trouble. I had a friend who did that, so I ignored her and got a new friend.
Jennifer, age 10, NJ

2. You lie all the time. You make up stories about yourself so that you can impress your friends or get out of trouble with your parents. If somebody finds out the truth, you make up a lie to cover it up. You've tried to control your lying, but it's a bad habit you can't seem to break.

...and then I said...

What would you do?

☐ a. Get control of yourself

I had that problem, too. Here's what I did: I told the truth once when I really wanted to tell a lie. It ended up feeling so good that I never told a lie again. Remember, you're in control of yourself and you can do anything you put your mind to.

Sara, age 11, PA

☐ b. Put it in writing

I used to have the same problem. Then I started writing in a journal. If you have a knack for overstating the truth, you could probably write on and on in a journal. It may be better to tell the truth in person and do the fibbing on paper. It worked for me!

Monica, age 12, TX

☐ c. Play it safe

Avoid getting into situations in which you think you need to lie.

Ariel, age 12, CA

3. You just found out that your sister smokes! You saw her smoking with a friend at the mall. One of your friends says that you shouldn't tell your parents because your sister would never forgive you.

What would you do?

☐ a. Confront your sister

This is going to be tough no matter what you do. First, you should talk to your sister and let her know that you saw her smoking. Tell her that if she doesn't tell your parents, you will. This gives your sister a chance to explain things to them.

Leah, age 11, CA

☐ b. Start a conversation

Some time at dinner, start up a conversation about smoking. Once my brother told me that he had smoked a couple of times, and when we had that conversation at dinner, he admitted everything to our parents.

Kristen, age 12, NY

☐ c. Tell your parents

No matter how angry your sister gets, it's important to tell your parents. Smoking can lead to serious lung disease, respiratory problems, and heart failure. If you tell your parents, maybe they can prevent your sister from becoming addicted.

Megan, age 14, OH

4.

■ One of your friends owes you $13. When you try to ask her for it, she laughs and ignores you. It has been a while, and you know she has the money. Now you owe your parents some money and need to pay them back.

What would you do?

☐ a. Be persistent

Don't let her get away with this! When she tries to change the subject, change it right back. Don't be rude or mean, but let her know that you mean business!

Julie, age 13, AZ

☐ b. Bill her

Even though you two are friends and you like to be generous, you have to draw the line somewhere. Give her a formal bill, and give her a week. If she doesn't pay up, start charging her interest.

Emily, age 11, CA

☐ c. Turn her in

Warn her that if she doesn't pay up, you will talk to her parents. If she still doesn't pay up, call her parents or tell your mom. And next time, don't lend her money!

Megan, age 11, OH

5. There is a girl in your class who is a little overweight. A lot of the boys call her names when the teacher is not around. You tell them that they wouldn't like it if they got teased, but they just say "Who cares?" or "Shut up."

What would you do?

☐ a. Stick up for her

These boys are total dorks, and you need to tell them who's who. Confront these boys, and don't let baby talk get in the way. "Who cares?" is an easy question to answer. Say, "I care, and I'm going to do something about this!"

Jessie, age 11, ME

☐ b. Help her help herself

It sounds as if this girl is afraid to stand up for herself. Maybe you can encourage her to tell those boys that she won't take the teasing. They will more likely listen to her than to you.

Nicole, age 12, MN

☐ c. Tell the teacher

What you are doing to stop these boys is nice, but if you really want to help this girl out, you should tell a teacher or another person in charge. They can take care of the problem.

Emily, age 12, NJ

Mostly **a**'s—Stand Up & Speak Out

You've got an opinion and you're not afraid to share it. You enjoy being a leader and fighting for what's right. Friends think you're intense, passionate, and self-disciplined. Other girls look to you when they're unsure of what to do. You can be loyal to those you care about. (For example, you'll talk *to* your sister rather than tell on her.)

It's easy for you to set boundaries with others and let them know how you feel. But how about when a friend disagrees with you? You've been known to overpower others when you feel they're challenging you. Work hard to have an open mind and really listen to other points of view. That way you'll earn not only the respect of your friends but their admiration, too.

Mostly b's—Creative Kid

You have the ability to see things from a unique perspective. When it comes to untangling even the most complicated problem, you usually come up with a solution. Creativity is your strength.

Others look to you because you're interesting, funny, and have something special to offer. But sometimes they might be intimidated by your creativity and confidence. Don't let them crush your spirit. Just remember to carefully choose where, when, and how you express yourself, and be open to others' ideas, too. Be sure you find ways to let your creative energy flow out. Write in a journal or make an art project that symbolizes what you're feeling.

Mostly C's—Better Safe Than Sorry

In a sticky situation, you opt to be safe, not sorry. When faced with a decision, you worry about doing the right thing and are quick to ask for help. You can be courageous when you have to be, like when ending a friendship you believe is harmful. But most of the time, you call on someone older and wiser to help you out of a jam.

Your parents look to you to be honest and trustworthy. But rather than look to them or someone else at the first sign of confusion, try giving yourself a chance to come up with a plan. If you run at the first sign of trouble, you might miss out on some really good friendships. So try to work through the small stuff on your own. It will help you prepare for the big stuff down the road.

School

You learn more in school than just English, science, or math. You also learn about dealing with others. Whether you're fighting with a friend or fighting for a better grade, you're learning to handle the pressure. School is your training ground for life. That's what makes it great. That's also what makes it hard.

1.

The girl who sits behind you in class always kneels on her chair to cheat off of your paper. She looks like she is stretching to see the board. How do you get her to stop without tattling?

What would you do?

☐ **a. Confront her**

Tell her to stop it. If that doesn't work, you'll just have to tell your teacher and ask her if you could be moved to another spot in the classroom.
Monica, age 14, CA

☐ **b. Help her study**

Why don't you ask her if she would like to study with you? Who knows? You might know more than she does on one subject, but she might be able to teach you a thing or two about something else. You might even become friends!
Katie, age 12, WA

☐ **c. Block her view**

Since you're not positive that she's really cheating, just try moving to a different seat or leaning over your paper to cover it up.
An American girl

2. You're starting middle school in September. You're really worried! You're afraid you'll get lost, get bullied, be late to class, or be unable to get your locker open!

What would you do?

☐ a. Plan and practice

I'm starting middle school, too. When I learn my locker combination, I'm going to write it down and put it in my backpack. When I get registered and know my classes, I will draw a map and write down when and where to go.

Beth, age 11, OR

☐ b. Stick with a friend

You could walk around with a friend for a few days. Then, if you get lost, you won't be so scared with her beside you.

Katie, age 10, FL

☐ c. Go with the flow

Remember that when you get to your first class, you'll be surrounded by 30 other kids who feel exactly the same way. And the lockers aren't going to work perfectly all the time. That's life!

Lisa, age 12, MI

3. You're a smart girl, but you're having problems getting motivated to finish all of your homework each night. So you're stuck doing it at school the next day.

What would you do?

☐ **a.** Stick to the schedule

To get motivated, you should set up an area where you do your work every day. It should include everything you'll need for your homework. When you get home from school, take a half-hour break to unwind. Then get to work! Do your hardest subjects first, then work your way down to the easiest ones.
Chloe, age 13, NY

☐ **b.** Find a study buddy

Get a friend to come over and help you, or go over to your friend's house and do your homework together!
Lennell, age 12, FL

☐ **c.** Take it easy

Don't do all your homework at once! Do a little bit and then play on the computer or watch TV. Maybe that will help!
Jenna, age 10, NY

4. You're in middle school now, and you have to shower and change after gym in front of the rest of the girls in your class. You're really modest, and this makes you very uncomfortable.

What would you do?

☐ a. Be quick about it

Try doing what you need to do as quickly as possible. Don't bother looking around to see what everyone else is doing. Just concentrate on what you have to do, and get it done.

An American girl, age 13, MA

☐ b. Get some help

Get a friend to hold a towel up in front of you so you can change in peace. Then do the same for her. This also works for taking showers.

Elizabeth, age 12, OH

☐ c. Get used to it

I know exactly how you feel. I still feel self-conscious, but after a week, I learned that no one cares. Everyone is very nice, and that makes showering after class easier.

Ellen, age 12, OH

5. Your ex-best bud started spreading rumors about how you are a selfish snob. It's not true! But now you walk down the halls and everyone says, "Oh, Ms. Snob is here." It hurts.

What would you do?

☐ a. Fight back

Talk with your ex-friend and tell her, "I am soooo NOT a snob that it isn't funny." Do it with people around her, so they'll hear what you say!
Rebecca, age 11, NY

☐ b. Call on your friends

You could ask some of your best friends to work together to let everyone know that you're not a snob. Since it won't be you talking, maybe people will pay attention.
Hannah, age 9, CA

☐ c. Pay no attention

Ignore the people who are bugging you and they'll get tired of it and stop. Whatever you do, don't spread rumors about your ex-best bud. This will be forgotten before you know it!
Megan, age 11, OH

Mostly **a**'s—On the Run

The good news is that when you face a challenge, you find a solution fast. The bad news is that sometimes you forget to think about others' feelings along the way. You try to do it all and do it all well. Your competitive nature spurs you on and gives you energy. So when you face a challenge, you get right to work on a solution.

While being the best and the brightest is your goal, be careful not to forget your friends and family. Remember that kindness counts. You don't have to be right every time for people to respect you and for you to be happy. If you're considerate of others along the way, your hard work and dedication will take you far.

Mostly b's—Buddy Up

You're into the latest trends and "who said what" at school. The faster you speed through your chores and homework, the quicker you can get to the computer or phone to chat with your friends. You're more than willing to help your buddies, and you turn to them when you're in a jam.

When things with friends are going well, you're on top of the world. But when there's trouble, it can hit you hard. Arguments at your house are usually about balancing homework and friends. Your friendships mean a lot to you, but you also need to make sure that your schoolwork is getting done (can you *really* get any homework done at your friend's house?). Remember, it's great to have friends, but it's also important to find a balance between studying and socializing.

Mostly C's—Chill Out

You like to live at a slow pace. You don't worry about the gossip at school. In fact, you might find it kind of boring. You're more content helping with the kindergartners or reading a book than listening to the latest at the lunch table. With homework, you sometimes procrastinate, and that can cause problems.

You prefer to avoid conflict. This works well for you most of the time— but sometimes, you have to step up and make a decision that isn't easy. Take time to think things through, and **don't shy away from what seems too hard.** Remember, going the extra mile can be worth it. So push yourself a little when you need to—you'll be glad you did.

Stressed Out

What does stress mean for you? Does it mean you need to lighten your load? Are you in need of some TLC or just confused about what direction to take next? Life can get overwhelming. But no matter what crisis hits, you're in charge of how you respond.

1. You worry too much. Your family says, "Stop worrying; it'll be O.K." Your friends tell you, "Don't worry about things." But you *are* worried! When you lie in bed, all your worries come back, and nothing your family or friends say helps.

What would you do?

☐ **a. Write it down**

I am the same way. Write your thoughts in a worry diary. Then write down a way that you can stop that worry. Any time one of those old worries comes up, look it up in your worry diary.
Jessica, age 12, MN

☐ **b. Call a friend**

This happens to me all the time. I normally call my friends and tell them about my worry, and then we start talking about something else. Soon I forget everything I was worrying about.
Emily, age 11, AL

☐ **c. Think happy thoughts**

Think about the good things happening right now. Try not to anticipate the problems of the future too much.
Thea, age 11, PA

2. Your friend's dad was very sick for a long time. He just died. You feel so bad for your friend, but you don't know what to say or if you should do anything for her. You don't know if she wants to talk. If she does want to talk, what should you say about her dad?

What would you do?

☐ **a. Make it, bake it, take it**

It can be hard to know what to do sometimes. When my friend's dad died, our class took lunches and made a scrapbook of all the memories we had of her dad.
An American girl

☐ **b. Let her grieve**

Ask your friend if she wants to talk. The best thing to talk about is all the good things her dad did. Tell your friend she can talk whenever she wants. When she's ready, she'll know she has a great friend to talk to and a shoulder to cry on.
An American girl

☐ **c. Take her mind off it**

When my dad died, my friend just came over and we hung out a lot. That really helped me get my mind off things. We just hung out and talked about normal stuff, and after a while we casually talked about my dad.
Jessie, age 12, NC

3. A few days ago, you got this really big pimple on your nose. Everyone at school has been staring at it. You washed your face every day, and you don't know what could be causing you to break out.

What would you do?

☐ **a. Cover it up**

Everyone gets pimples sometime, so don't worry. Consider yourself lucky that you have only one! For now, continue washing your face, and maybe ask your mom if you can buy some cover-up makeup until the pimple goes away.
Michelle, age 13, FL

☐ **b. Get some advice**

Everyone gets pimples. Talk to an older friend or relative about it. Ask what she did about having a pimple and how it made her feel around her peers. You'll get great answers and advice.
Alma, age 11, IL

☐ **c. Forget about it**

Just forget about your face and concentrate on how you act! Your real pals won't care anyway.
An American Girl

4. You're afraid to go to the doctor! You don't like getting shots or having your finger pricked. You're afraid that you'll cry and look like a baby, even though you're in fifth grade.

What would you do?

☐ a. Get informed

Talk to the nurse about what will happen at your appointment. You won't feel as scared if you know what is going on. Don't be afraid to ask questions!
Lauren, age 10, WA

☐ b. Lean on Mom

If you have to get a shot, turn your head and ask your mom or dad if you can squeeze her or his hand. That's what I do.
Diana, age 13, VA

☐ c. Laughter is the best medicine

Start a funny conversation with your mom so that you will be smiling, and the shot won't hurt as much.
Sara, age 13, FL

5. The start-of-the-school-year dance is coming up soon. You're new to the school, and you don't really want to go to the dance because you don't feel comfortable yet. There's just one thing: your parents are making you go! They say it will be a good way to make new friends. You've tried telling them you don't want to go, but they won't listen.

What would you do?

❑ a. Help out

Help with refreshments or take money at the entrance. You'll meet all the kids in your new school, and if you work with other kids who are doing the same job as you, you'll get to know them, too! At our school dances, I work the refreshment stand all the time, and I have more fun than some of the kids who are dancing!
Rachel, age 14, PA

❑ b. Strike a deal

I think you should meet your parents halfway. Go to the dance, but see if your parents will agree to let you call home and ask to be picked up if you don't like it.
Laura, age 12, OR

❑ c. Grin and bear it

Things like this happen to me a lot. Just go. You might end up liking it more than you thought.
Jennifer, age 13, MI

Tally your answers here:

a's_____   **b**'s_____   **c**'s_____

Mostly a's—Busy Bee

When you're stressed, the first thing you do is get busy! You're practical and steady on your feet. When the road gets rocky, you spring into action. You're a natural leader. In a crisis, you're not likely to get emotional. Instead, you look for what is within your control, and you go about getting it done.

When you *do* get a little nervous, you dive in and get informed—just knowing what is going on is usually enough to calm you down. Try to reach out when you're hurting or feeling blue. Don't be afraid to ask for guidance or reassurance. Part of being truly strong is knowing when to ask for help.

When you're stressed, you reach out. Your friends think you're a good listener and look to you for comfort. Your ability to both communicate and listen to others will take you far. Adults love your inquisitive nature. When you're not sure about something, you ask. You're likely to get several opinions and pick the one that works best for you.

Be careful about how much you say, who you share things with, and what you put into e-mail to friends. Because you are so skilled at expressing yourself, you also open yourself up to being betrayed. Try using a journal and putting your most private thoughts in writing.

Mostly C's—Distraction Action

Your motto: think positive! You always look at the glass as half full. Avoiding conflict whenever you can, you put things out of your mind rather than deal with them head-on. When a friend is in need, you'll most likely distract her from her troubles instead of talking about the troubles themselves. Your gift is that you don't take yourself (or anything else) too seriously. It takes a special person to joke about a pimple—on her own face!

But sometimes you *will* have to talk about things. If you avoid dealing with tough issues, you might miss out on getting closer to someone. Worse yet, you could lose someone's respect, because you didn't take her seriously. Slow down, take time to look at difficult situations, and be sure to ask for help if you need it. It might be hard at first, but you'll be glad you did.

Some Last Thoughts

Now you know a bit more about how you approach life in general and how that outlook helps you solve your problems in school, at home, and with your friends.

Whatever your style—go-getter, go-with-the-flow, or somewhere in between—here are some important points to think about when you're solving problems or making choices. Sometimes even a small shift in thinking can make a big difference.

Remember, your life is the result of choices you make. Try to make the ones that are best for you.

Big Truth 1
Problems don't fix themselves.

Sometimes you may get away with sweeping a problem under the rug, but most of the time, if you avoid dealing with a problem, your feelings will come out in another, less positive way, which can affect your relationships—even your health.

Bottom line: **Take charge.** Look for a solution and try your best to make it happen.

Big Truth 2
There are many ways to solve a problem.

Solving problems is like trying on clothes—one size doesn't fit all, even if the solutions are all good choices. What might be good advice for one girl would never work for another.

Above all, **be open to different approaches.** The goal is to find a solution that everyone involved can live with. Keep your mind—and your heart—open to new ideas.

Big Truth 3

Resist the temptation to be hurtful.

When you're angry or hurt—or just feel like you have no control over your life—spreading the pain around might seem like a good idea. But being hurtful always creates more problems than it solves.

Instead, take a different approach—call it **"taking the high road."** Don't give in to name-calling, spreading rumors, backstabbing, or other kinds of revenge. You'll gain respect from the people around you and you'll be much happier with yourself.

Big Truth 4

Listen to the voice inside you.

In your busy life, sometimes you need to stop and look at the direction your life is taking. Spend some time alone to listen to the wise voice inside that helps you make good decisions.

Above all, **be honest with yourself.**

Big Truth 5
Speak up. Say what's on your mind.

What you think matters. But people can't know how you feel if you don't tell them. **Be respectful, but be clear.**

If someone's trampling on your view of the world, let her know it's not O.K. Think about it: If *you're* not in your corner, who's going to be?

YOU can do it!

Finally, remember that nobody's perfect. You will make mistakes. There will be times when you feel as if your life's been turned upside down, when it's hard to convince yourself that you really are O.K. This happens to everybody; it's part of life. That's when you have to tap into your strengths and get support where you can. Then hang on and ride out the storm.

But always, always be proud of the girl you are. Look at each decision made or problem solved as a small victory.

You can't prepare for every situation, but if you listen to your heart, trust your instincts, and speak your mind, you'll be ready for just about anything that comes your way.

Write to us!

Have you ever been in a difficult situation? What tough choices have you had to make? Tell us how you solved a problem.

Write to us at
What Would YOU Do? Editor
American Girl
8400 Fairway Place
Middleton, WI 53562

Or visit our Web site at **americangirl.com**.